MY FIRST SCIENCE TEXTBOOK

Electrons

Written by Mary Wissinger

Illustrated by Harriet Kim Anh Rodis

Created and edited by John J. Coveyou

Science, Naturally!
An imprint of Platypus Media, LLC
Washington, D.C.

My First Science Textbook: Electrons
Copyright © 2021, 2016 Genius Games, LLC
Originally published by Genius Games, LLC in 2016

Written by Mary Wissinger
Illustrated by Harriet Kim Anh Rodis with Uzuri Designs
Created and edited by John J. Coveyou

Published by Science, Naturally!
English hardback first edition • 2016 • ISBN: 978-1-945779-01-5
        Second edition • June 2021
English paperback first edition • September 2021 • ISBN: 978-1-938492-48-8
English eBook first edition • 2016 • ISBN: 978-1-945779-07-7
English board book first edition • 2016 • ISBN: 978-1-945779-04-6
Bilingual (En/Sp) paperback first edition • September 2021 • ISBN: 978-1-938492-49-5
Bilingual (En/Sp) eBook first edition • September 2021 • ISBN: 978-1-938492-50-1

Enjoy all the titles in the series:
        Atoms • Los átomos
        Protons and Neutrons • Los protones y los neutrones
        Electrons • Los electrones

Teacher's Guide available at the Educational Resources page of ScienceNaturally.com.

Published in the United States by:
        Science, Naturally!
                An imprint of Platypus Media, LLC
        725 8th Street, SE, Washington, D.C. 20003
        202-465-4798 • Fax: 202-558-2132
        Info@ScienceNaturally.com • ScienceNaturally.com

Distributed to the trade by:
        National Book Network (North America)
                301-459-3366 • Toll-free: 800-462-6420
                CustomerCare@NBNbooks.com • NBNbooks.com
        NBN international (worldwide)
                NBNi.Cservs@IngramContent.com • Distribution.NBNi.co.uk

Library of Congress Control Number: 2021936483

10 9 8 7 6 5 4 3 2 1

Printed in Canada

Expand and extend the content in this book with our extensive Teacher's Guide.
Available for free download at ScienceNaturally.com.

I'm Ellie the Electron,
a particle with class.

I'm negatively charged
and have very little mass.

I'm attracted to the proton.

I'm almost 2,000 times smaller than it.

More electrons could fit on this dot

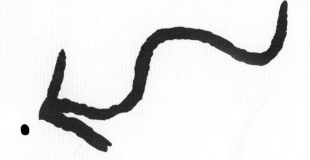

than there are people on the planet.

Population–7.7 Billion

Pick which you'd like to calculate—
my speed or my location.

You can't know both at once.
It's an uncertain situation.

HEISENBERG UNCERTAINTY PRINCIPLE

$$\Delta x \Delta p \geq \frac{h}{2\pi}$$

Look around this room;
see anything that's glowing?

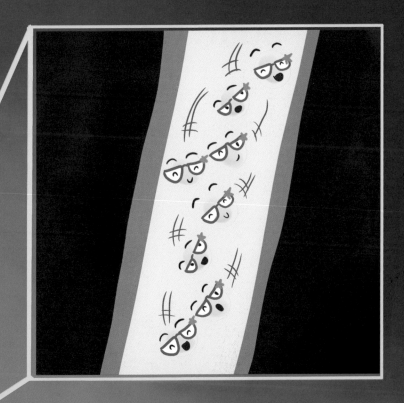

If it's powered by electricity,
that means electrons are flowing.

When it's cold and dry in winter, electrons build up when you walk.

Touch something
and I'll jump to balance out.

You'll feel a static shock.

Electrons are mysterious,
and we change how we behave.

Watch close
and we act like particles.

Observed
Double Slit Experiment

24

Turn your back
and we act like waves.

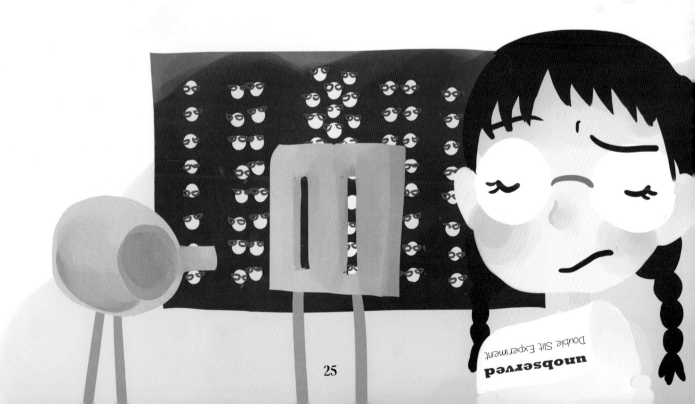

25

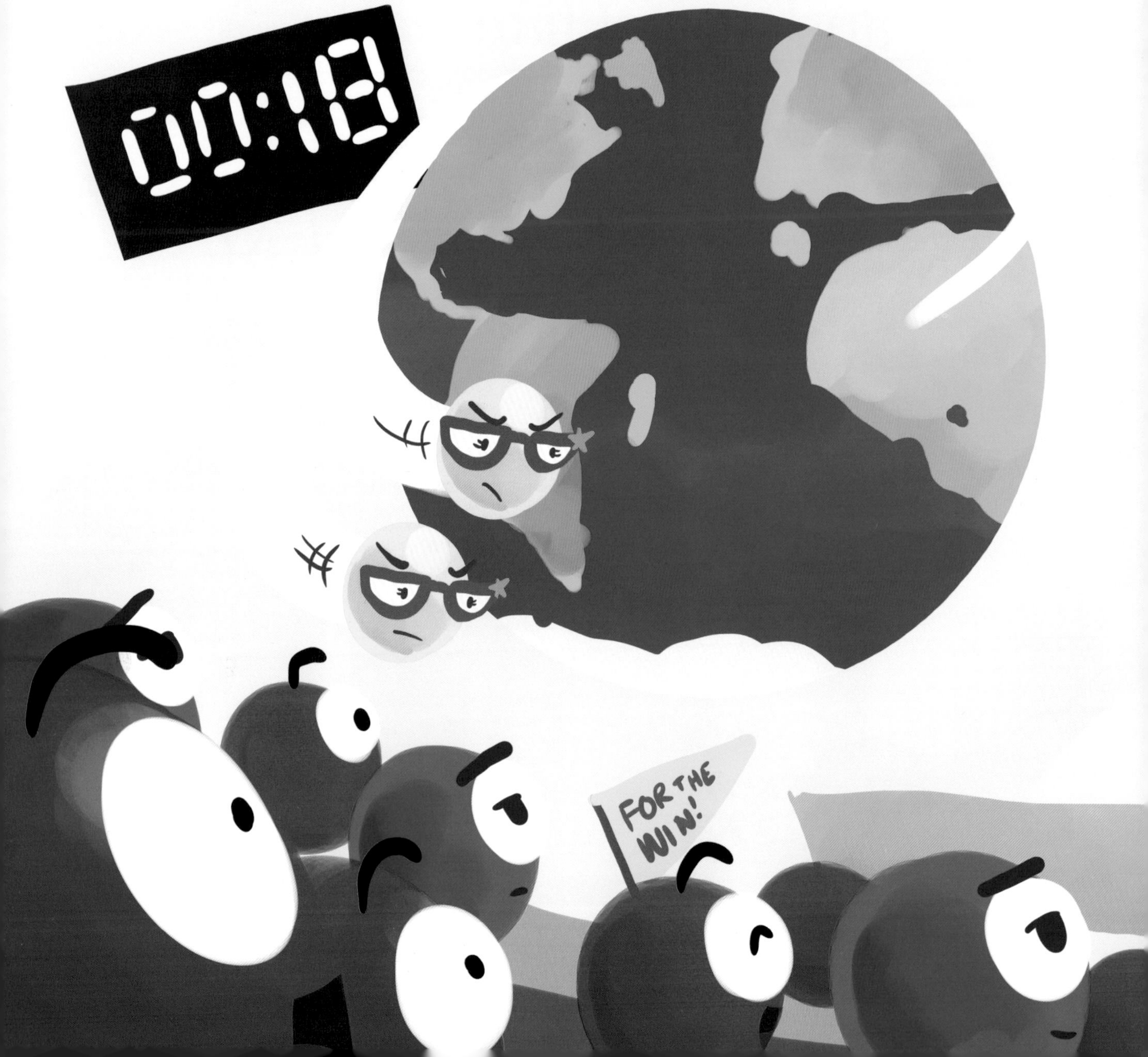
00:18
FOR THE WIN!

If we were in a race, we could circle the world in eighteen seconds.

Electrons are a part of the atom, but we are subatomic legends!

Glossary

ATOMS: The building blocks for all matter in our universe. They are so small that you can't see them, and are made up of even smaller particles called protons, neutrons, and electrons.

DOUBLE SLIT EXPERIMENT: A demonstration showing that electrons can act like both waves and particles at the same time—a concept known as wave-particle duality.

CHARGE: An electric charge is a property of matter. There are two types of electric charges: positive and negative. Protons have a positive charge and electrons have a negative charge.

ELECTRICITY: A type of energy created when electrons move from one atom to another in the same direction. Electricity is the flow of electrons.

ELECTRONS: Very teeny particles with a negative electric charge. Electrons travel around the nucleus of every atom.

HEISENBERG UNCERTAINTY PRINCIPLE: A rule discovered by physicist Werner Heisenberg, which tells us that the location and the speed of a particle, like an electron, can't be measured at the same time.

MASS: A measure of how much matter is in an object. Mass is different from weight because the mass of an object never changes, but its weight will change based on its location in the universe.

NEUTRONS: Very teeny particles with no electric charge, found in the nucleus of most atoms.

NUCLEUS: The center of an atom, made up of protons and neutrons.

PARTICLES: Tiny, singular bits of matter that can range in size from subatomic particles, such as electrons, to ones large enough to be seen, such as particles of dust floating in sunlight.

PROBABILITY: Probability is the likelihood that something will happen. It is impossible to know exactly where an electron will be inside an atom, because electrons are always moving very fast, but scientists can calculate the probability of an electron being in a certain area. An atomic orbital, or electron cloud (pictured as the ring around the nucleus), is the part of an atom where an electron is likely to be.

PROTONS: Very teeny particles with a positive electric charge. Protons are in the nucleus of every atom.

STATIC SHOCK: When an object or person has a negative charge from extra electrons, and they touch an object that has a positive charge from too few electrons, electricity jumps between the two. You might feel a static shock when you touch something made of metal.

SUBATOMIC PARTICLE: A particle that is smaller than an atom and exists within it, like protons, neutrons, or electrons.

WAVES: A repeated up-and-down pattern of movement that lets energy travel from one place to another. Sound waves, light waves, and ocean waves are examples of different types of waves.

Discover the
My First Science Textbook series

Book 2

Book 1

MY FIRST SCIENCE TEXTBOOK
Atoms

Written by Mary Wissinger
Illustrated by Harriet Kim Anh Rodis

MY FIRST SCIENCE TEXTBOOK
Protons and Neutrons

Written by Mary Wissinger
Illustrated by Harriet Kim Anh Rodis

Book 3

MY FIRST SCIENCE TEXTBOOK
Electrons

Written by Mary Wissinger
Illustrated by Harriet Kim Anh Rodis

Protons and Neutrons:
Hardback ISBN: 978-1-945779-00-8
Paperback ISBN: 978-1-938492-45-7
Bilingual (En/Sp) ISBN: 978-1-938492-46-4

Atoms:
Hardback ISBN: 978-1-945779-02-2
Paperback ISBN: 978-1-938492-41-9
Bilingual (En/Sp) ISBN: 978-1-938492-39-6

Electrons:
Hardback ISBN: 978-1-945779-01-5
Paperback ISBN: 978-1-938492-48-8
Bilingual (En/Sp) ISBN: 978-1-938492-49-5

8 x 8" • 32 pages • Ages 2-7
Hardback: $14.99 • Paperback: $12.95
Also available in eBook and board book!

Science, Naturally!

Sparking curiosity
through reading

ScienceNaturally.com
Info@ScienceNaturally.com